Puppy Training 101:

Everything You Need to Train Your Dog at Home,
Including Step-by-Step Directions, Solutions to Common
Problems, and Suggestions for Training Older Dogs

Kimberly Mays

Digital Print House

Acknowledgments

I would like to recognize, acknowledge, and applaud all the people around the world who helped make this book and this mission possible. I cannot name you all by name, but you know who you are. I am honored to serve with you on this noble mission of educating the world and helping each individual become a better person today than they were yesterday.

I would like to specifically highlight and mention those individuals who were directly instrumental in the writing and publishing of this book: my husband for his encouragement, my children for their patience, and my lovable mutt Dixie for testing the research with me.

Table of Contents

Introduction

Whether the pet is a long-time part of the family or a brand new addition, most families have no idea how to train their dogs. Untrained puppies become unruly dogs. Many dog owners find themselves with a dog they cannot control or understand. Have you ever seen an otherwise-friendly dog neglected or abandoned because the owner could not get the dog to stop barking, chewing, or running away? Or what about the dog whose owners do not notice terrorizing visitors and other dogs at the dog park? The good news is that very few dogs are beyond help! Successful training does not need to be expensive or difficult. In this book, I will show you how to easily and effectively train your puppy to be a calm, helpful member of the household.

Using my personal experience with dogs from a young age and cutting-edge research from respected scientific journals, I will give you the information and confidence you need to establish and maintain positive expectations with your puppy. My association with family pets has improved my own life, and I want each dog and dog family to experience that same joy. It breaks my heart to see previously adored puppies left outside all day or dropped off at the local pound because the owners do not know how to train their dog.

Training a puppy is a relatively simple process that requires more time and patience than sophistication. Even if you have never trained a dog before, you can achieve success by following the suggestions in this book. Training your dog has never been simpler!

Dog training need not cost an arm and a leg. By following the suggestions in this book, you can train your own puppy *at home*!

A calm and well-behaved dog can improve your quality of life. The key to a successful training program is to start small and be consistent. Do not wait! You and your dog both deserve the chance to work together. Imagine in your mind's eye the relationship you would like to have with your dog—hiking together, relaxing on the porch, or playing Frisbee in the park without him running off the other way. Give your puppy the chance he deserves to prove how much he can learn. You can achieve this level of success if you start now.

Chapter One

Before You Begin

Positive rewards will reinforce what you are teaching your dog. Rewards can (and should) come in many forms!

Understanding Your Relationship to Your Dog

Dogs are unique in the animal kingdom because of their ability to read and respond to human emotion. While dogs share many characteristics with their canid relatives, wolves, there are significant differences between the species. Miklósi et al. (2003) found that dogs and socialized wolves respond differently to human gestures and commands. The dogs in the study were also more likely to look to the humans for approval and help.[1] Training methods that depend heavily on the hierarchy of wolf packs, for example, may be overlooking the unique relationship between dogs and their human families. A successful training plan will be built on leadership, consistency, and rewarding positive behaviors.

Leadership: Your dog will look to you for guidance and expectations. Be assertive with your dog, especially when it comes to where he can go in the house and the behaviors you find acceptable. It is important to remain calm, however, as your dog will take his cues from your tone and mood.

---

[1] Miklósi, Á., Kubinyi E., Topál, J., Gácsi, M., Virányi, Zs., Csányi, V. (2003) A simple reason for a big difference: wolves do not look back at humans but dogs do. Current Biology 13: 763-766.

Consistency: It is crucial to establish consistent boundaries with your dog. That consistency should extend to all members of the family and behavior with strangers and guests. If some family members let the dog on the couch and others scold him for the same behavior, your dog's obedience will suffer for that inconsistency. It is also important to maintain the same rules with guests and family members. If you allow your dog to jump up to greet you after work, it is unrealistic to expect him to stay down when guests arrive.

Rewarding positive behaviors: You will train your dog to repeat desired behaviors by rewarding him when he does something good. Positive rewards will reinforce what you are teaching your dog, whether it is a trick or following a house rule. Rewards can (and should) come in many forms: praise, play, affection, sound cues, or treats.

Rewarding Positive Behaviors: Should You Use Food and Treats?

Professional dog trainers and animal experts are divided when it comes to the question of whether or not to use food rewards when training your dog. Proponents of biscuit training say that it is an easy way to tie desired behaviors to positive stimulus. Treats are a quick and convenient way to reward your dog both in the early stages of training and as you move to reinforcement and practice. Trainers and owners who oppose food-based training claim that relying on treats will teach your dog to respond only for food, which can lead to inconsistent obedience. A compromise that many trainers make is to begin training with treats and then replace the food with other, non-food rewards.

Here are some considerations to keep in mind when dog training with treats or food rewards:

1. *Be generous with your rewards.* Dog training is not the time to be stern or stingy. You may need to give multiple treats for new skills. For example, you may use a treat to guide your dog's nose up when teaching him to sit. When he begins to crouch down, offer him the first treat. Once he is sitting, give him another. If you opt to train your dog with treats, you will find the most success if you are generous with them.

2. *Use smaller treats more frequently.* When you think of a dog treat, you may be imagining a large biscuit or tender meat-flavored chew. In reality, you can achieve the same benefit with small pieces of dry dog food or a portion of a dog biscuit. The main purpose of treat training is to reinforce positive behaviors. The more you reinforce the desired behavior, the more often your dog will repeat the action. Giving small treats will keep the training treats from derailing your dog's diet and allow you to reward him more often.

3. *Combine treats with praise.* Whether or not you plan to wean your dog off food rewards, always praise your dog verbally when giving him a treat. Doing so will condition him to associate your verbal praise with positive behaviors. The words themselves do not matter as much as your tone. Some popular choices are "Yes!,' "Good dog!," and "Okay!"

4. *Be quick with the treat.* One mistake new dog trainers make is waiting too long to offer the reward. It is common to see a dog rewarded for sitting right as he stands up. All this does is confuse your dog. Is he being rewarded for sitting or for standing? Reward your dog when he is in the middle of the desired action. If you want your dog to walk calmly by your side, give him a treat or two during the walk any time he is doing just that. If your dog runs from you and you call him back, reward him for coming back. Scolding him at that point will not teach him not to run; it will teach him to fear coming back.

5. *Do not wean your dog off the treats too soon.* If you want to work away from food rewards, start by combining treats and other rewards. Praise, play, and affection are powerful rewards in their own right. When your dog responds correctly to commands eight out of every ten times in a variety of situations, you can begin weaning him off treats. Replace the food reward with extra praise or affection one out of every three times. If his obedience does not suffer for the reduction, you can continue reducing the frequency of the treats.

6. *Do not give up treats completely.* Even after you wean your dog off food rewards, a treat can offer powerful reinforcement. During your regular training practice, give yourself permission to offer a treat for spectacular performance. It will not take many treats to keep your dog behaving in hopes for another similar reward.

Clicker training uses a similar conditioning technique, although the dog is being conditioned to associate a sound with the reward.

You can purchase a small training clicker online or at any pet store, or use another sound (even a word works!). The actual sound matters less than how it is used. Clickers are a preferred tool for many dog trainers because they are small, precise, and easy to use. Here are some tips for incorporating clicker conditioning into your obedience training:

1. *Start by teaching your dog that a click means a reward.* Begin clicker training with a pocketful of treats. Click the clicker with one hand while offering your dog a treat from the other until your pocket is empty. Even if you do not intend to use food rewards at any other point, giving your dog a treat or small piece of dry food while you click will teach him that a click accompanies a reward.

2. *Respond quickly.* When you move on to obedience training, click when your dog completes the task (or even a partial task if teaching complicated skills). One of the advantages of clickers over other positive reinforcement is that it takes next to no time to respond. Click the instant your dog turns his head or moves his body where you want it. Speed is important; your dog is learning to associate specific actions and positions with the click and reward.

3. *Combine a click with another reward during early training.* When you move to obedience training, combine a click with another reward. This can be a treat, although many trainers use clickers to avoid conditioning their dogs to food-based rewards. Give praise, affection, treats, or another reward each time your dog completes the task. Your praise will be his primary conditioning and the click will be a secondary one.

The power of two-tiered conditioning is what makes clicker training so effective.

4. *Continue to reward skills after mastery*. Many dog owners take for granted that their dogs will respond to commands after initial training. While a click and treat is not necessary every time, take a moment to praise and pat your dog when he responds. Periodic reinforcement of good behaviors with a click and reward will go a long way to keeping your dog eager to please.

5. *Use the clicker only for reinforcing desired behavior.* Once your dog associates the click with a reward, he will naturally snap to attention when he hears a click. Upon discovering this connection, some dog owners will use the clicker to get their dogs' attention or pull them away from temptations. Your dog will become confused if a click does not accompany a skill or behavior you are trying to teach. Resist the temptation to use your clicker in any other way! When your dog can no longer rely on the clicker, it will lose its effectiveness.

What You Need Before You Start

Make sure you have the following supplies before you begin training your dog. The items on this list are mentioned in the book and will help you in your training experience. Items marked as optional are suggested depending on the training style that you choose to employ.

- Wire dog crate

- Carpet shampoo

- Timer

- Collar with ID tags

- Extendable leash (or multiple leashes of varying lengths)

- Chew toys

- Frisbee/ball/toys for playing fetch

- Chest harness or head collar

- Small treats (optional)

- Clicker (optional)

- Training discs or rattle bottle (optional)

In addition to the aforementioned items, prepare yourself by practicing patience. Lasting training takes time and energy, but do not let that discourage you. The result will be worth the effort!

Chapter 1 Takeaways

1. Dogs have evolved to look to humans for guidance and cues. They are more in tune with human emotion than any other animal.

2. A successful training plan will be built on leadership, consistency, and rewarding positive behaviors.

3. Treats and other food rewards are powerful motivators you can use to teach new skills and reinforce desired behavior.

4. Combine treats with praise and affection. This will make the reward more powerful and give you the option to wean off food rewards down the road.

5. Consider clicker training if you are looking for a way to train your dog that does not depend on treats.

Chapter Two

Specific Considerations Based on Age and Breed

Most aspects of training your dog will be the same regardless of the type of dog you bring home. Some details will vary depending on the age and breed of dog; knowing these particulars can be helpful in creating a more successful and rewarding training environment.

When to Begin Training

You should start to teach your dog basic home rules and routines right away. House training and simple commands can be taught to puppies as young as eight weeks of age. Keep in mind that very young dogs have short attention spans; training should take place in short sessions (five minutes or less) throughout the day. Aim for a higher frequency of sessions rather than a longer duration.

In addition to simple commands and house training, puppies should be socialized at a young age. Once your dog has his first round of vaccinations, he can begin limited socialization with other dogs. Hold off on trips to the dog park until your dog has all of his vaccinations (usually around four months of age).

Most experts suggest beginning formal training when your dog is between 3-6 months of age. Waiting until after six months can allow bad habits to form; formal training before three months is impractical because of the puppy's attention span and physical capabilities. If you do end up starting obedience training with a dog older than six months of age, refer to Chapter 8 for more information.

Consider the Breed

Dog breeds are sometimes divided into classifications based on personality and tendencies. While most aspects of training your dog will be the same regardless of the type of dog you bring home, knowing the particulars of your dog's group can be helpful in preventing frustration and diagnosing any problems. For the purposes of training techniques, six groups to remember are retrievers/pointers, spaniels, protectors, herders, hounds, and terriers.

Retrievers/Pointers: Originally bred to be hunting companions, most retrievers and pointers are highly trainable and eager to please. Their loyalty makes them great companions, especially for children. They are very active and need lots of exercise. Most breeds love to swim and play fetch by instinct. Their desire to be around people and high energy can cause them to turn to digging and chewing if not properly exercised. Example breeds include the standard Poodle, Golden Retriever, German Shorthair Pointer, Weimaraner, and Labrador Retriever.

Specific training considerations: Retrievers and Pointers are high-energy and eager to please. This can sometimes translate to a jumpy, over-eager dog. Training will be more successful if you exercise your Retriever first. This will burn off some of the excess energy and encourage calm patience. Another tip to keep Retrievers and Pointers from destructive chewing is to give them plenty of toys and bones to chew. Direct their natural "mouthiness" away from the couch and toward an acceptable chew toy.

Spaniels: Spaniels are some of the gentlest dog groups. Their calm and gentle demeanors make them very good with children. They are playful, fun, and adventurous. Many spaniels are successfully used as outdoors or hiking companions. Their long coats require regular grooming. Example breeds include the English and American Cocker Spaniel, Brittany, and Cavalier King Charles.

Specific training considerations: Use a calm voice and gentle direction when training your Spaniel. If you're too aggressive, the dog's gentle nature can be a disadvantage, leading to submissive urination, whining, or biting out of fear.

Protectors: Most protector breeds have been bred specifically to defend or guard people. They are athletic, intelligent, and loyal. By necessity, they are very trainable, although their temperaments depend on breeding. They are naturally wary of strangers but are gentle with those they consider family. Most dogs in this group are large and strong. Example breeds include the German Shepherd, Boxer, Rottweiler, Great Dane, Buffmastiff, and Doberman Pinscher.

Specific training considerations: Give your puppy plenty of opportunities to socialize with people and other dogs at a young age. This will keep your dog from becoming overly hostile or aggressive. Be firm and consistent when training. Avoid physical discipline or yelling, which can cause dogs in this group to respond with aggression because they are so in tune with your emotions. This same attention to your mood can be a benefit in training; a firm "no!" should be enough to stop any undesirable behavior once consistent training has begun.

Herders: Herding and other livestock dogs are bred to be working animals. As a result, they are extremely intelligent and independent. They will chase big game, including cars. They will bark at intruders and can sometimes be nippy, especially those varieties bred to herd cattle and larger livestock. Herding dogs most often have thick coats for staying warm outdoors year-round. Common examples include the Collie, Queensland Heeler, Louisiana Catahoula Leopard Dog, Corgi, and German Shepherd.

Specific training considerations: Once trained, herding and livestock breeds are some of the most capable. They can be taught complicated tasks off-leash and are obedient at long distances. That same independence and intelligence can make initial training difficult, however. They are often bored and need regular work to keep them busy. These breeds need ongoing socialization to keep them from getting too territorial. It is very important to teach them to come on command for times when they start chasing large animals or vehicles off the property.

Hounds: Often bred as hunting dogs, hounds make loyal companions. They are quiet inside but can bay very loudly when left alone in the yard. They are gentle, adventurous, and kind. Depending on the variety, they are very sensitive to scents (scent hounds) or prone to chasing small animals to keep them in sight (sight hounds). Breed examples include the Greyhound, Beagle, Basset Hound, Coonhound, and Dachshund.

Specific training considerations: Because of their breeding as hunting dogs, most hounds will follow the scent or sight of prey for long distances. They require gentle training. Introduce distractions slowly for the most consistent training; too many sights or scents at once will make training very difficult. Most hounds will never do extensive off-leash work because the urge to chase is just too strong.

Terriers: These often-small dogs are easy to care for and make great family companions. They can be defiant and stubborn without proper training. Terriers were originally bred as hunters, so they have a strong chase impulse. If not worked or trained sufficiently, they are prone to digging and chewing. They often respond to threats by snapping and nipping. Most terrier coats require special grooming. Example breeds include the Jack Russell Terrier, Yorkshire Terrier, Scottish Terrier, and Schnauzer.

Specific training considerations: Maybe because terriers are often small breeds, many terrier owners are not as consistent with training and rules as owners of large breeds. The stereotypical aggression and defiance of some terriers may come back to this lack of consistency. Be firm but gentle with your dog. Offer rewards for positive behavior and avoid physical punishments, which can encourage aggression.

Understanding your dog's group can help you understand his motivation and prominent character traits. This understanding will be helpful when training and enjoying your pet. Not all dogs within a breed or breeds within a group will have the same personality, however. In addition to specific variation, many dogs are a combination of two or more breeds. In most cases, mixed-breed dogs will have milder representations of the tendencies of their different breeds.

Chapter 2 Takeaways

1. Start teaching your dog the house rules and routines right away.

2. If possible, begin formal training when your dog is between 3-6 months of age.

3. All dogs are trainable, but breeds are bred for different purposes. The history of your breed will explain many of your dog's behaviors.

4. Refer to your dog's breed group for specific suggestions that can help with training.

5. Mixed-breed dogs often exhibit the best qualities of their different breeds.

Chapter Three

Training Basics

Short, regular training sessions combined with a strong bond with your dog will make training an enjoyable experience for both of you.

Why Bonding Is Important

Many dog owners assume that their dog's love and trust are automatic. While it is true that dogs are naturally affectionate, a strong bond between dog and owner takes work. Nurturing your bond with your dog has many benefits for you and the dog. Your dog will be easier to train, listen more attentively, and be calmer overall when he feels secure in his relationship with you. Bonding with your dog is not just good for your dog—your quality of life will improve as well. Research supports the common idea that dog ownership, especially when a strong bond exists between the dog and owner, has positive physical and emotional effects.[2]

The good news is that the important work of bonding with your dog can be easy and enjoyable! Use one (or all) of the following suggestions to strengthen your bond with your dog:

1. ***Talk to your dog.*** Talking to your dog is a great way to bond. Many dogs understand quite a few words, and dogs have been shown to read body language and tone better than we do. Your dog will be able to pick up on your mood and may even

---

[2] Knight S. & Edwards V. (2008) In the company of wolves: the physical, social, and psychological benefits of dog ownership. J Aging Health 20:437-455.

help improve it. Dogs make a great, nonjudgmental sounding board.

2. ***Be consistent.*** Your dog will be calmer and better behaved if he is sure of the rules. Consistency in your expectations and routine will help him feel secure in his place. Scheduling walk- and mealtimes will be good for you both.

3. ***Play together every day.*** Puppies especially love to play. Make time each day to play fetch, toss around a Frisbee, or teach him a new trick. Nothing will build a bond faster than good, old-fashioned play.

4. ***Look him in the eye.*** Research has shown that looking your dog in the eye strengthens the bond between owner and pet. Meeting gazes causes an increase in oxytocin levels (a hormone that promotes nurturing and attachment) in both the dog and his owner.[3]

Keep It Short

Many short training sessions will be more successful long-term than the same practice crammed into one marathon session. Young dogs especially benefit from shorter training sessions with frequent breaks. This is not to say that training should be done five minutes at a time each day. A study by Demant et al. (2011) indicated that the ideal training schedule for retention is twice a week, with each training session broken up into smaller chunks of

[3] Nagasawa, M., Mitsui S., En, S., Ohtani, N., Ohta, M., Sakuma, Y., Onaka, T., Mogi, K. & Kikusui, T. (2015) Oxytocin-gaze positive loop and the coevolution of human-dog bonds. Science 17:333-336.

time.[4] Aim for 4-5 sessions of 10 minutes (or shorter if your dog loses interest) twice a week. This will allow you to plan training around your work and travel schedule while allowing your dog time to rehearse the training during sleep.

The primary goal in training should be to reinforce positive behaviors, both with rewards and consistency. Mistakes and defiance are more likely when your dog is physically and mentally exhausted. Be consistent in your training while giving your dog time to rest. The dogs in the Demant et al. study (2011) all learned the commands over a four-week period, but those that were trained twice a week in a higher number of shorter sessions acquired the skills faster and with less resistance.

Reading Your Dog's Body Language

Training will be more successful when you and your dog are both relaxed and happy. An overly stressed or nervous dog will not learn or perform well, leading to bad habits and frustration. Look for the following signs of your dog's mood:

Relaxed: When your dog is comfortable, he will stand with his head high and his legs loose. His tail will be down and relaxed. Any tail movement will be a gentle sway. His tongue may be lolling out of his mouth because his mouth will be open slightly. Some dog breeds even appear to be smiling when they are happy. This is the ideal state for training.

---

[4] Demant, H., Ladewig, J., Balsby T.J.S. & Dabelsteen, T. (2011) The effect of frequency and duration of training sessions on acquisition and long-term memory in dogs. Applied Animal Behaviour Science 133:228-234.

Playful: A dog that is feeling playful will have a hard time holding still. His tail will be up and wagging, often so quickly that his entire backside wiggles. He may be moving toward you or he may lean forward while bending his front legs. He will often bark or jump toward you by way of invitation. In this state, your dog is ready to run and play. He will be too wound up to pay proper attention. Spend a few minutes playing before attempting to calm him down.

Curious/alert: Any new smells or situations will cause your dog to enter this state. He will assess the situation and determine if the environment is friendly. Most dogs will point their ears up and forward when curious or alert. He may cock his head to one side. He will stand firmly, leaning forward slightly. His tail will be up but not stiff. A dog will not stay in this position for long. Once your dog has evaluated the potential threat, he will either relax or prepare to fight or flee.

Aggressive: When your dog responds to potential threats with aggression, his tail will be stiff and his hair may seem to stand on end. He will curl his lips so his teeth are visible. He may or may not accompany this stance with a growl.

Submissive: A submissive or fearful dog will often make his body small in order to appear non-threatening. His tail will be down and may curl under his body. He will lower his body and lay his ears back. He will not maintain direct eye contact and may only peer out of the corners of his eyes, exposing mostly the whites. He may lick at the dominant person or dog to show submission.

Learning to read your dog's body language is one of the best ways to be sure he is ready to learn a new skill or practice training. Use your own body language and tone to help your dog be relaxed and attentive before attempting any training. This will go a long way to preventing a negative training session.

Practice Makes Perfect (or Pretty Close to It)

Consistent practice is the only thing that will take your dog from a place where he obeys when he feels like it to where he obeys every time. Dedicate a short time during training for practicing commands and skills. Regular reinforcement is key.

Professional dog trainers recognize three factors that contribute to the difficulty of obedience success (known as the 3 D's): duration, distance, and distraction. Strengthen each of these areas one at a time with each command you teach your dog. When teaching your dog to come when called, for example, gradually call to him from farther and farther away. You will know you have reached his limit when your dog stops responding. Get closer and practice with him at the edge of his distance limit. When you are ready to introduce duration or distraction, cut the distance back to an easy level. For example, introduce distraction by calling him to come outside or while someone else is making noises at home. Gradually increase the distraction. You will know you have reached mastery when your dog will respond at the dog park or while chasing a squirrel. If a distraction proves to be too enticing, reduce the distractions until you find the point where your dog will respond every time. Spend more time practicing and rewarding his response before attempting to increase the difficulty.

Practice is not just for new skills! Even a well-trained dog will benefit from periodic reinforcement with whichever reward method you choose. Practice is especially helpful after a major change (such as a move or the birth of a child) when your dog may have slipped into some bad habits.

Practice is good for you too. Do your best to keep your voice and response consistent when you correct or praise your pup. Because the situation and environment you ask your dog to obey in will inevitably change, maintaining a reliable response will help your dog understand what you expect.

Chapter 3 Takeaways

1. Nurture a healthy bond with your dog by playing with him and spending time together.

2. A strong bond with your dog can also improve your quality of life!

3. Dogs are the only animals (other than humans) for which eye contact encourages loyalty and affection.

4. The best training schedule is twice a week for 30-45 minutes, broken up into four or five shorter sessions.

5. Learn to read your dog's body language. Doing this will let you know what he is thinking and when is a good time to work on training and manners.

6. Practice new and old skills regularly.

7. Remember the 3 D's of difficulty: duration, distance, and distraction. When working on one factor, reduce the difficulty of the other two.

Chapter Four

Getting Started

The first routines and commands you teach your dog are very important. There is no easier time to set consistent boundaries than the first days of training.

Establishing Routines

When you first bring a puppy or new dog home, it is natural to want to begin training right away. Before you begin with specific commands, however, it is important to help your new dog fit in your home and family routine. A new place full of unfamiliar smells can be frightening for a dog. The following home rules and routines will make the transition easier for everyone:

1. ***Where to find food and water.*** Introduce your dog to his water and food dishes. Plan to feed your dog at the same time(s) each day for the first week. This will help him learn the feeding routines to expect.

2. ***Where to sleep.*** If you plan to crate train your dog, have the crate set up and ready when you bring him home. Wherever you plan to put your bed to sleep, consistency is key. What starts as a one-night exception to let the dog into your bed can easily become an every night occurrence.

3. ***Where his toys are.*** Your new dog may not learn to put away his toys for some time, but knowing where to find interesting toys will help keep him out of your things. Pick a spot in the

house to store his toys and show him where to find them the first day.

4. *Where he can (and cannot) go in the house.* Before bringing your dog home, decide where he will be allowed to go. Be sure that everyone in the house knows if you plan to keep him out of certain rooms or off the couch.

5. *NO and YES.* The first words your dog should learn to recognize are "no" and "yes." When you are playing with your dog or he does something good, reward him with petting, praise, and an upbeat "yes!" Conversely, when you remove your dog from an area you do not want him or correct him in another way, accompany the action with a firm, "no!" Some dog owners also choose to associate "no" with a rattling noise given off by training discs or an empty bottle filled with loose gravel.

The First Four Commands

Once you are ready to begin teaching specific commands, start with the most versatile and basic. The following four commands are a great place to start with your dog because they are useful in all kinds of situations. It does little good to have a dog that will roll over on command if he will not even come when you call.

Sit: Most dogs will naturally lower themselves into a sitting position when their noses are up in the air. Encourage your dog to look up by holding a treat close to his nose and then slowly raising your hand. When he is in a sitting position, say "sit" before rewarding him with praise and the treat. Repeat the process 2-3 times when first starting to teach the command.

Reinforce the skill by having your dog sit before he eats or goes out on a walk. This reinforcement has three benefits: your dog will be calm while you prepare for the meal or walk, he will begin to associate the command and your verbal praise with the pleasures that come after, and he will learn to sit on command.

Come: Teaching your dog to come when called is similar to teaching him to sit. Start teaching the command when your dog is already wearing his collar and leash. Pull gently on the leash while saying, "come" and looking directly at your dog. When he gets to you, praise him and give him a treat (if applicable).

Once your dog has mastered this step, begin taking a step backward when you call him. Step away slowly, tugging on the leash very gently, until he catches up with you. Be sure to give him a treat and tell him what a good job he has done! Training him to come even when you are moving away will also help encourage polite behavior on walks.

Gradually increase the difficulty as he masters the command. Continue practicing and reinforcing the training with increasingly longer leashes until you and your dog are ready to work on the command without the help of a leash. The goal is to work your way up to a place where your dog will come on command even in a noisy dog park or when he would rather be chasing after a squirrel.

An important part of teaching your dog to come on command is associating the behavior with fun, positive results. Although it can be useful to have a dog that will come for a bath or come back after slipping out the door, be sure to praise your dog in an upbeat tone whenever he obeys. Even if you need to follow the command up with something unpleasant, do not forget the immediate praise. This will keep the dog from learning that "come" means he is in trouble.

Stay: There are times when you will need your dog to stay where he is instead of following after you or an interesting scent. The basics of teaching your dog to stay are simple, although the experience can be more challenging in practice. Puppies and energetic breeds especially struggle with staying put for long.

Start by telling your dog to "stay" while holding your hand out, palm down. Reward your dog for staying put after just a few seconds. If you are using treats in your training, quickly offer the treat to him on the ground near his paws. Holding the treat above him will only encourage him to get up. Gradually increase the length of time that you wait before giving your dog a treat.

Do not forget to teach your dog a release command! Choose a word and gesture that will signal to your dog it is time to get up and move freely. You will eventually give this command before any treats or praise so that your dog learns the reward comes *after* he waits. The word you choose does not matter, although some trainers recommend choosing something you are not likely to say in an average conversation to clear up any potential confusion. Whatever you decide, say it in a clear and upbeat voice so your dog will form positive associations with the word and gesture.

The same principles apply when teaching your dog to stay while you walk away. Once he has mastered the art of staying for more than a few minutes, begin introducing more distance or distraction. Begin teaching him to stay while you back a few steps away rather than turning your back. Adding distance will make the time you ask him to stay put seem longer than when you are standing close by, so praise him quickly until he gets the hang of staying when you leave the area.

Leave It: Teaching your dog to turn away from something interesting is an important safety measure. When you do this properly, you will be able to stop your dog from eating something he should not, such as trash or something hazardous.

At the beginning stages, you will need two treats. Some trainers suggest using a dry dog biscuit for one treat and a soft, meaty treat for the other. Place one treat (the dry biscuit if you use more than one type) on the floor and cover it with your foot. Your dog will probably attempt to get the treat from under your foot. When your dog turns away or backs off slightly, praise him and reward him with the other treat. It is very important that you not give him the treat under your foot. You are trying to teach him that your reward will be better than whatever is on the floor. Holding the first treat in one hand and the other treat behind your back is another, similar arrangement.

As he learns to turn away from the first treat, begin increasing the difficulty and introducing the verbal cue. Place the treat on the floor next to your foot. This will allow you to cover the treat if needed. When your dog turns away or looks to you expectantly, say, "Leave it!" and reward him with praise and the second treat.

Once your dog has a handle on what you are asking him to do, say, "Leave it!" when you place the treat on the ground or hold it out in your hand. At this point, you can work through progressively more difficult situations: better treats, more distractions, or outside of the home.

Chapter 4 Takeaways

1. Establish basic routines early.

2. Feeding and walking your dog at the same time every day will help him adjust to the household schedule.

3. Set aside a place for your dog to sleep and for his toys.

4. Decide where (and where not) in the house the dog will be allowed to go. Be consistent with these boundaries.

5. Start your dog's training with four basic commands: sit, come, stay, and leave it.

Chapter Five

The Case for Crate Training

Dogs instinctively adapt well to crate training because a comfortable crate becomes a private den where your dog can relax.

Most dogs naturally seek out a private, enclosed area to function as a safe resting place. Dog crates and kennels are designed to provide a den-like space where dogs can rest without getting in the way or into trouble. You will likely find that your dog often retires to his crate by choice. That's because no matter how strange it seems to us, dogs love their crates! Crate training is especially helpful when housebreaking a puppy because dogs will instinctively do what they can to keep their sleeping place clean and dry.

Choosing the Right Crate

The crate should be just large enough for your dog to stand up with his head raised and turn around without hitting the sides. A crate that is too small will be uncomfortable for your dog. A crate that is too large can lead to your dog soiling a corner of the space, eliminating the advantage crate training can provide for housebreaking. If you are purchasing a crate before your dog is fully grown, choose a crate that will accommodate your dog's adult size. Some crates even feature a movable back wall so you can adjust the size of the crate as your dog grows.

Most crates are made from either plastic or wire. Plastic crates usually have solid or partially solid sides, providing a private enclosure for your dog. Wire crates offer better ventilation and are usually easy to collapse for storage when not in use. Choose the material that best fits your lifestyle and living space; either style will suit your dog's needs just fine.

The Dos and Don'ts of Crate Training

DO make the crate comfortable. Line the crate with a bed or soft blanket. When you introduce your dog to the crate, do so in a non-threatening way. Leave the door open and let the dog explore the crate with you nearby. Put the crate out of the way in a common room of the house so your dog will feel part of the action but still have a quiet place to retreat when he needs a break.

DO introduce a verbal command. Tell your dog to enter the crate with a reliable command such as "crate" or "kennel." Point to the crate with a treat in your hand and reward him with the treat when he goes to the crate.

DO feed your dog in the crate. Feeding your dog inside his crate will help him feel comfortable there. If your dog will not enter the crate voluntarily, begin by feeding him right next to the crate. As he develops positive associations with the crate, gradually move the food a little farther inside the crate at each meal. Eventually, your dog should enjoy his meal with the bowl at the very back of the crate.

DO increase the amount of time your dog spends in the crate gradually. Start by closing the door while your dog eats. Open the door and let him out as soon as he finishes his meal. Sit nearby or in the same room as you increase the amount of time he spends in the crate. If he begins to whine while in the crate, do not let him out until he is calm.

DO put your dog to bed in the crate. The crate should feel like home to your dog. Teach him to sleep, rest, and relax inside his den. As mentioned earlier, do not let your dog out when he whines. If your dog needs a bathroom break or is awake and ready to play, let him out when he is calm and quiet. Letting him out of the crate while he is whining is similar to rewarding him for whining.

DON'T use the crate as a punishment. Your dog's kennel is his place to relax. You will not be able to take advantage of the benefits of crate training if your dog views the crate as a negative place. If you punish your dog by locking him in the crate, he will begin to fear it.

DON'T leave your dog in the crate too long. A general rule of thumb is that a puppy should be physically able to control his bladder for one hour for every month old he is. After your dog is physically capable of staying in the crate, you should still be careful not to leave him in there longer than necessary. Your dog will still need plenty of exercise and interaction! If you leave the crate door open, your dog may choose to come and go throughout the day.

Chapter 5 Takeaways

1. Crate training gives your dog a quiet place to rest and somewhere you can leave your dog when you cannot supervise him.

2. Choose a crate that is large enough for your dog to turn around, stand up, and raise his head comfortably.

3. Introduce your dog to the crate gradually.

4. Do not use the crate as punishment or leave your dog in the crate longer than he can handle comfortably.

Chapter Six

House Training

Housebreaking your puppy will take some time and effort, but it does not need to be a difficult or stressful experience!

House training your puppy will be much easier once you have introduced him to his crate. Most dogs will do their best to avoid soiling the place they sleep. When your dog has a full bladder, he will probably begin to whine or scratch at the crate. If you give him plenty of opportunities to do his business outside of his crate, his natural desire to keep the area dry will help you teach him when and where to go.

Establish a Reliable Routine

The long-term benefits of getting your puppy on a schedule are plentiful. A schedule helps your dog understand where and when he is permitted to empty his bladder. It will also be helpful when you need to leave your dog for the day, especially if you have trained him to go before and after work. Take your puppy outside often, but especially first thing in the morning and right before bed. After meals and after waking up from a nap are good times as well. He may not eliminate every time, but he will grow accustomed to having the opportunity. This will make it easier for him to wait indoors.

It can also be helpful to feed your dog at the same time every day and take your dog to the same spot outdoors each time. Pick a word of phrase to associate with potty trips. Say the word while he is relieving himself. Eventually, you will be able to use the time, place, and word to encourage him to go when you choose.

Reward Success Promptly

As with all other training goals, be sure to reward your dog when he successfully does his business outside. Be generous with your praise and treats. He will begin to associate outdoor elimination with positive rewards. Be sure to reward him immediately after he is finished. If you wait until you go indoors, he may think you are rewarding him for going inside. That is not the behavior you want to reinforce! Do be sure to let your dog finish his business before rewarding him, however. Offering a treat or enthusiastic praise before he is done is likely to distract him from finishing the deed.

Give Freedom Gradually

A common mistake in new dog owners is allowing your puppy too much freedom as soon as he makes any progressing in housetraining. Just because a dog will often relieve himself outside does not mean he is ready for free reign of the house. Keep your puppy close by so that you can watch for signs that he may need to go outside. When you cannot stay close at hand, confine him in his crate for short periods. Be sure to take him outside as soon as you let him out of the crate. Housebreaking your puppy will take some time and effort, but it does not need to be a difficult or stressful experience.

Be Patient

Even the most careful training will not prevent all accidents. Remember to be patient with the process. Punishing a dog for eliminating in the house will not do anything other than confuse him. If you catch him in the act, interrupt him and take him outside immediately. If you find evidence of an accident, clean it thoroughly. Dogs will often use scent to return to a previous site to relieve themselves, so it is important that you use a cleaner designed to remove all odors. If your dog is having regular accidents indoors, you may have been giving him too much freedom too soon.

Chapter 6 Takeaways

1. Teach your dog when to empty his bladder by setting a feeding schedule and taking him outside regularly.

2. Be generous and consistent with your praise (and a treat) whenever your dog does his business outside.

3. Keep your dog close at hand throughout the training process. Too much freedom too soon will lead to accidents around the house.

4. Do not scold him for mistakes. Take him outdoors immediately to finish his business.

5. Use odor-blocking cleaner on any accident indoors to keep your dog from using the scent to guide him back to the same spot.

Chapter Seven

Grooming and Gentleness

With some basic training, you can teach your dog be gentle and stand patiently for grooming.

Dog training should not just be limited to getting your puppy to sit or come on command. Grooming and interaction with other people and animals will be regular events in your dog's life. Set him up for success by teaching him how to patiently handle grooming and gently interact with others.

Teach Your Dog to Stand Still for Grooming

There are many reasons you will want your puppy to handle grooming calmly. If your dog ever sustains an injury or gets a cactus thorn stuck in his paw, for example, you will want to be able to help him without him shying away from the process. The basics of teaching your dog to hold still for grooming are the same as obedience training: start small, be generous with praise, and practice.

1. *Start small.* Do not expect your dog to hold still to have his nails trimmed right off the bat, especially if your dog has had any negative experiences with grooming. Instead, start by conditioning your dog to hold still and offer you a foot. Work your way up to the point where your dog patiently tolerates the nail trimmer tapping against his nails. It may take a few minutes or a few days to get to this point, depending on the temperament or experiences of your dog. Follow a similar

schedule for other grooming needs. Before you brush your dog's teeth, get him used to you holding his head near the mouth.

2. **_Be generous with praise._** Being touched and groomed can be stressful for some dogs. Help your dog develop positive associations with patiently sitting still through the grooming process by rewarding him generously. Offer your dog small treats while you brush him and handle his feet and head. Erring on the side of extra praise will help you teach your dog that grooming is a positive experience.

3. **_Practice._** The more often you practice with your dog, the more comfortable he will be. Aim for short sessions (2-3 minutes long). This will keep your dog from tiring out or developing a negative association with the process. Practice with him often, at different times of day and in different rooms. The ultimate goal is that your dog will be comfortable during vet visits or if any grooming is necessary away from home.

How to Reinforce Gentleness

Puppies must be taught to be gentle. Dogs are naturally playful and often roughhouse as part of their regular play. It is also instinctive for most dogs to be possessive of their food and territory, but that does not mean you should fear your dog. With some basic training, you can help your dog be gentle with people and other animals alike.

1. *Spay or neuter your dog.* There are many reasons to have your dog spayed or neutered. Just one benefit is that your dog will calm down after the procedure. He will be less interested in projecting dominance and be easier to handle. This is especially important for male dogs, although even female dogs have been shown to be calmer after the surgery.

2. *Do not play rough.* Some trainers suggest that tug-of-war and other physical games teach a dog to be rough. If you do play tug-of-war with your dog, lay some ground rules first. Teach your dog to release the toy on command by relaxing your grip while still holding the toy. When your dog releases the toy, praise him and say your verbal cue (such as "drop it"). Reward him with praise and a treat. In time, he will learn to drop the toy when you give the command. If your dog is too rough or fails to observe any of the ground rules, simply stop the game. Prematurely ending the game will quickly teach him that he can only enjoy your company when he is gentle.

3. *Use treats to teach gentleness.* Train your dog to take treats gently. This will come in handy when rewarding him for obedience and also give you the opportunity to introduce a verbal command for gentleness (such as "gentle" or "easy"). Offer your dog a small treat or piece of dry dog food, saying your verbal cue as you extend your hand. If your dog nips or is rough when taking the food, do not let him have the treat. If he approaches it gently, praise him and give him the treat while saying your chosen cue. In time, this will teach him to associate gentleness with positive rewards.

Chapter 7 Takeaways

1. Train your dog to hold still for grooming with the following tips: start small, be generous with praise, and practice often.

2. Short, regular training practice is more effective than one long session.

3. Establish ground rules before playing tug-of-war or other rough games with your dog.

Chapter Eight

Walks and Leash Behavior

If you find your dog still will not listen or you want to reinforce your position as head of the pack, take more walks together! A daily or twice-daily walk is a great time to strengthen your bond with your dog and reinforce key training principles.

Taking a daily walk with your dog is a great way to get exercise—for you and for your dog! Many dog owners avoid regular walks, however, because of behavioral problems that may arise when their dogs are around new smells, people, and animals. Take the time to establish good walking habits and you will find the benefits spill over into your dog's behavior the rest of the day.

Make Walks a Priority

One of the best ways to train your dog to walk politely is to take regular walks. Many behavioral problems stem from dogs being overly excited and undertrained. Schedule a regular time for walking your dog each day, even if that means waking up an hour earlier to fit in the walk. A walk after dinner or after work is a great time to stretch your legs and help your dog work off any pent-up energy or anxiety from the day. In addition to the health benefits, regular walking will reinforce your position as the leader of the pack. If you do nothing else, try increasing the number of walks you take together. Regular exercise and practice on the leash will make a huge difference in how your dog behaves while out and about.

Stop Pulling and Lunging

Understanding why your dog pulls at the leash can be helpful in correcting the behavior. When a dog pulls or strains at the leash, excess energy is often to blame. Before trying to fix the behavior, be sure that your dog has had an adequate opportunity to run off any extra energy. This can mean letting your dog play outside before the walk or starting your walk with a jog. Another reason that dogs pull at the leash is their inherent curiosity. Even walks around the block are full of sights and smells your dog will want to investigate. Allow your dog some time to sniff and explore, using "come" or "let's go" when you are ready to move on. Some dog owners find breaking up the walk with time at an off-leash dog park can help curb some of the urge to wander.

Once your dog is settled and well exercised, encourage him to stay close to you by keeping the leash short. Slowly increase the length of free lead as long as your dog continues to walk at your pace. If he begins pulling on the leash again, stop walking until the pulling stops. Once the leash is relaxed, continue walking again at the same pace as before.

It can be helpful to spend some time training proper leash behavior somewhere familiar, such as the backyard or inside the house. Practicing leash etiquette at home reduces the number of distractions and allows you to spend a short, concentrated time on the desired behavior. Put on the leash when you take him outside to use the bathroom. Get your dog to follow your lead by taking a few steps in the yard or around the house; offer praise and change directions each time your dog follows. If he begins to pull on the leash, immediately turn and walk the other way. Each of these activities will help your dog associate the leash with following your lead.

If your dog continues to pull on the leash after thorough exercise and consistent training, you may want to purchase a collar or harness designed specifically to discourage pulling. The most common varieties include a chest harness and a head collar.

Chest harness: Look for a harness that includes a ring near the dog's chest for attaching the leash. Chest harnesses redirect the momentum of a pulling dog backward, reducing much of the force you will feel when your dog lunges. Harnesses are especially helpful for dogs much stronger than the person doing the walking and for very small dogs, whose tracheas can be injured by traditional collars when they pull or lunge. Select the brand and size that securely fit your dog without chafing. Easy Walk is a popular brand available at most stores nationwide.

Head collar: Head collars fit around the muzzle and neck. The lead attaches to a ring under the dog's chin. The collar is designed to tighten slightly across the muzzle when the dog pulls at the leash, discouraging lunging and jumping. Head collars do not restrict the dog's ability to eat, drink, or pant. Gentle Leader is a name brand of this type of collar. Head collars are especially useful for dogs with small heads relative to neck size.

Use Walks to Reinforce Training and Bond

Your daily walk is a great time to reinforce the training your dog is working on at home. Practicing your commands in a new environment will be challenging for your dog—there are so many distractions when out for a walk! For the best results, spend just a few minutes at a time on commands and focus on basic training first. Be quick and generous with your praise. If your dog is just too distracted to work, try again later in the walk.

Strengthen your relationship with your dog by walking together regularly. Talk to your dog on the walk. Praise him for good behavior. The goal is to keep your dog focused on you throughout the walk. If you interact with him and show him affection and praise when he earns it, he will behave better. Check to see if your dog is looking up at you periodically throughout the walk. Walking at your pace and looking up at your face are signs your dog considers the walk a shared experience.

Chapter 8 Takeaways:

1. Regularly walking your dog has many health benefits for you and the dog.

2. Make regular walks a priority by establishing a walking routine.

3. Practice proper leash behavior at home when you first begin training.

4. Choose the right equipment if you need additional help keeping your dog from pulling or lunging.

5. Use walk time to reinforce training and bond with your dog.

Chapter Nine

Troubleshooting Common Problems

Most negative behaviors stem from boredom, fear, or excess energy.

Q: How can I keep my dog from barking all night?

A: If your dog is barking all night, he may be bored or under-exercised. In addition to providing more stimulation throughout the day, find a way to break the pattern when he starts barking. Interrupt him with a word or sound, then encourage him to lie down and relax.

Q: Help! How do I teach my dog to stop jumping on guests?

A: Your dog is probably jumping on guests out of enthusiasm. The best way to stop this behavior is to teach your dog that he will not get attention when he jumps up. When your dog jumps, do not acknowledge or look at your dog. Simply turn your head and body away. He will quickly learn to seek attention with another behavior.

Q: Why is my dog uninterested in treats?

A: Most of the time, when a dog shows no interest in treats, it is because he is already full. Rather than leaving your dog's food out all day, consider feeding him twice a day. After twenty minutes, remove any food he has not eaten.

Q: How can I wean my dog off of treats?

A: Some specific suggestions for moving away from treats are outlined in Chapter One. In addition to those ideas, remember that a treat is not the only way to reward good behavior. Your attention and affection is a powerful reward in its own right.

Q: My housetrained dog pees when excited or nervous. What can I do?

A: What your dog is doing is called submissive urination. Do not reward the behavior by interacting with your dog when he pees indoors. Help him get more comfortable with the house and routine by speaking calmly and eliminating possible stressors.

Q: Why is my dog digging in the yard?

A: Dogs dig when they are bored or hot. A resting spot a few inches below the surface of the yard is often cooer. One option is to designate part of the yard where you are okay letting your dog dig. Another option is to make sure that he gets plenty of exercise and mental stimulation. Consider filling a Kong toy with treats or vegetables frozen inside to keep your dog entertained and cool throughout the day.

Q: My dog will sit but will not stay. How can I teach him to stay put longer?

A: For information on increasing the duration of any particular skill, refer to Chapter Three. You may also have success varying the length of time you ask him to sit. Dogs are aware of our habits we may not have even noticed. It is possible that you are always asking him to sit for the same length of time and he is responding to the habit.

Q: How do I train an older dog?

A: Training an older dog is not much different than training a puppy. Two main differences are that an adult dog is physically capable of more and that you may need to undo any bad habits your dog has learned previously. Start small, be consistent, and reward your dog generously. It may take longer for him to understand what you want, but your dog will move to mastery quickly once he does.

Determine the Source of the Problem

No matter what undesirable behavior you would like to fix, understanding the root cause will make your remediation easier. Most negative behaviors stem from boredom, fear, or excess energy. If you find your dog reverting out of previously trained behaviors or skills, evaluate how you interact with your dog. Are you still rewarding him periodically for doing what you ask? Have you been rewarding the wrong moment? Do what you can to assess the situation before deciding how to fix the problem.

Chapter 9 Takeaways

1. Most behavioral problems can be fixed with proper exercise and patient training.

2. To stop unwanted jumping or submissive urination, turn away from your dog when he jumps or urinates. He views interaction with you as the ultimate reward.

3. Understanding the root of your dog's training issue will help you resolve the problem.

One Last Thought

Whether you are starting with a brand new puppy or working with an old family pet, you can train your own dog at home. Training is a great chance to build a bond with your dog. Why spend good money so someone else can develop that relationship?

There is nothing so sad as a family pet abandoned for behaviors that can easily be corrected with basic obedience training. Successful training does not need to be expensive or difficult. You can teach your own dog with nothing more than the information in this book and your love for your pet.

Training a puppy is a relatively simple process that requires more time and patience than sophistication. Even if you have never trained a dog before, you can achieve success by following the suggestions in this book. Armed with the information included, you are ready to get to work--training your dog has never been so easy or rewarding!

Can You Help?

I'd love to hear your opinion about this book! In the world of book publishing, there are few things more valuable than honest reviews from a wide variety of readers.

Your review will help other readers find out if my book is for them. It will also help me reach more readers by increasing the visibility of my book.

About the Author

The author's earliest memories are of trying to teach her dog to understand commands in Pig Latin. (It didn't work.) Since then, she has fallen in love at first sight with any puppy that wags its tail her way. She lives with her husband, children, and pets on three acres perfect for playing fetch. This is her first book on dog training.

Made in the USA
Middletown, DE
30 December 2016